Seeds of Well-Being Poems

Five Steps for Staying Constructive in the
Face of Change and Challenge

Kent Burnett, Ph.D.
Margaret Crosbie-Burnett, Ph.D.

DEDICATION

We dedicate this book to our children, their spouses, and our grandchildren, with the hope that its message will promote constructive attitudes and actions in their lives, and to the memory of our parents and grandparents whose love, care, and sacrifices set us on our current path.

PREFACE

In this book we bring together ideas derived from ancient philosophers, contemporary research findings from the social and behavioral sciences, and nearly 80 years of experience in psychology between us, including research, teaching, clinical practice, and supervision of trainees. The result is a concise, simple to follow book that explains our five-step method for staying cool and constructive in the face of change and challenge. Poems accompany each of the steps and are intended to make learning about the five steps more fun and memorable.

The material in this book is designed for teens, adults, and seniors who wish to learn to get a "better grip" on non-constructive emotions and make mindful choices that better reflect who they are when they are their "best self." On whatever paths you find yourself in life, we hope that the methods described in this book will help you to stay as constructive as possible.

CONTENTS

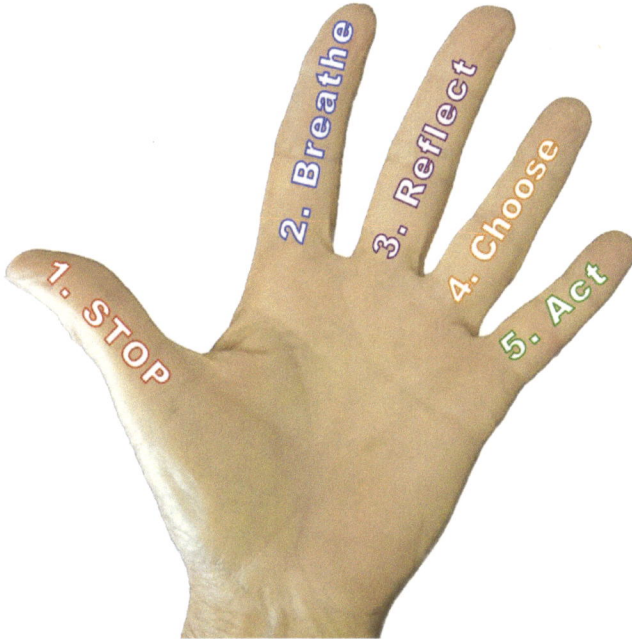

STAY COOL—BE COOL

We created the *Seeds of Well-Being Cool Hand* as the centerpiece of our five-step method for shaping one's life when adapting to change and challenge. The *Cool Hand* uses the five fingers of your left hand to help you remember these steps. The five sequenced steps are: **Stop**, **Breathe**, **Reflect**, **Choose**, then **Act**. The steps are designed to help you increase

1

your ability to **Stay Constructive** or **Return to Being Constructive** in challenging situations. When no immediate threat to your own or others' basic safety or security exists and no immediate response is demanded, it is generally wise to **Stop** or **Slow Down**, center yourself emotionally and physiologically, and reflect on your options for responding constructively.

As with any hand, the fingers of the *Seeds of Well-Being Cool Hand* are separate but not totally distinct from one another. For some tasks a single finger of the *Cool Hand* is sufficient to help you adapt constructively; for example, sometimes it is enough just to **Stop** doing something that is hurtful or **Choose t**o take a small risk to do something that makes you uneasy—but is clearly constructive.

However, when adapting to more challenging situations, in which the path to constructive action is ambiguous or involves unfamiliar tasks, all of the fingers of the *Cool Hand* may need to work together to keep you constructive in your actions. When the entire *Cool Hand* is skillfully coordinated, it can help you "get a grip" on even the most demanding challenges.

The *Seeds of Well-Being Cool Hand* can be used in a variety of situations, for example:

- You find yourself in an ambiguous situation and are not sure what to do.
- You are anxious or worried about an upcoming event or change in your life.

2

- You have to make a difficult choice or decision.
- You find yourself becoming irritated or withdrawing emotionally.
- You are anticipating a happy change in your life, but you know that it will create challenges.

The following sections of this book describe each the five steps of the *Cool Hand*. Poems accompany each of the steps and are intended to make learning about the *Cool Hand* more fun and memorable.

It Matters

There are times
when it is wise
to attack, run, or hide

But otherwise
Think things through
It matters what you do

STEP 1: STOP!

STOP!

暂停
ストップ
Subsisto
Σταματήστε
रुकिए
توقف
הפסק
Hættu
Kuacha
그만
Stopp
Rete
Dừng lại
หยุด
Arrêtez
Alto Fermati
Pare
Cron
Halt
Prestani
Berhenti
Dur
Itigil

STOP before you CRITICIZE

STOP before you INTIMIDATE

STOP before you RIDICULE

STOP before you VIOLATE

STOP before you HARDEN YOUR HEART

STOP before you SURRENDER TO HATE

STOP before you CROSS THE LINE

STOP before it is TOO LATE

STOP and RE-EVALUATE...

J ust as in driving a car, the ability to **Stop** is adaptive in life. Remember that slowing down and calming yourself does not mean that you are slow or unable to act; it means that YOU—rather than your emotions—are in command of what you will do next.

Here is what we suggest in order to help you refine your ability to **Stop** before acting non-constructively. In stressful or confusing situations, when no immediate action is required for the safety, security, or survival of self or others, take time to **Stop** or **Slow Down**. This is an important first step in order to prevent saying or doing something that may be an overreaction, irrational, an expression of momentary emotions, or regretted later. If you are with others, you may need to look away, turn away, or even move to another physical space. If the situation requires you to explain your behavior, you might say something like, "I need a minute." That is better than saying something negative or non-constructive.

Thought-stopping is stopping or interrupting or slowing your ongoing "thinking behavior." **Stop** and listen to your thoughts, which are also called your internal monologue or self-talk. Your thoughts may be critical of yourself and/or others, or even critical about the world in general. In any case silently say, "**Stop!**" to yourself.

When you have stopped your actions (including talking, and your internal monologue), which may be non-constructive, quickly turn your attention to breathing in order to calm, steady, and ready yourself for constructive action. If you are tired or hungry, or needing to attend to other bodily needs, it is important to attend to those needs as well.

GO FIGURE

When something is not the way you want
Do your emotions run away with you?
Or do you calmly figure out what to do?

STEP 2: BREATHE

BREATHE

Nature demands that we breathe
And mostly we do it with ease
But when we are stressed, angry, or blue
It takes effort to keep the air moving through

When you're at risk of losing your cool
Remember to follow this simple rule:

Breathe slowly...
Breathe deeply...
Breathe completely...

深呼吸	Kupumua	Respirare
深呼吸する	심호흡	Respira
Spirant	Pust	дышать
Αναπνεύστε	Respire	Atmen
सांस लो	Thở	Diši
تنفس	נושם	Bernafas
לנשום	Respirez	Nefes
Andaðu	¡Respira	Huninga

U nder normal circumstances, we breathe in a nearly effortless manner in concert with the pace of our activity, just as the waves, pictured in the Breathe poem, move toward the shore and then retreat rhythmically. However, when we are under stress, angry, or anxious, our normal pattern of rhythmic breathing can become rapid and shallow, irregular, halting, or incomplete.

When you notice that your breathing has changed in any of these ways, it is important to restore your breathing to full efficiency, bringing it back into concert with your activity level. This is an essential first step toward calming your physical self and quieting your mind, so that your potential for clear thinking, wise decision-making, and constructive action is maximized.

Breathing serves many critical functions, one of which is to help you stay poised under pressure. Remember to monitor your breathing to ensure that you are breathing slowly, deeply, and completely. Whenever you notice that your breathing is rapid, halting, uneven, or shallow, we suggest that you use the final stanza of the Breathe poem as a mantra to help you stay poised or, if necessary, to regain your composure. You can repeat this mantra to yourself, either aloud or silently, as a self-instruction as often as needed for as long as needed and anywhere you happen to be, to help you maintain or regain your Inner Calm.

Breathe slowly...

Breathe deeply...

Breathe completely...

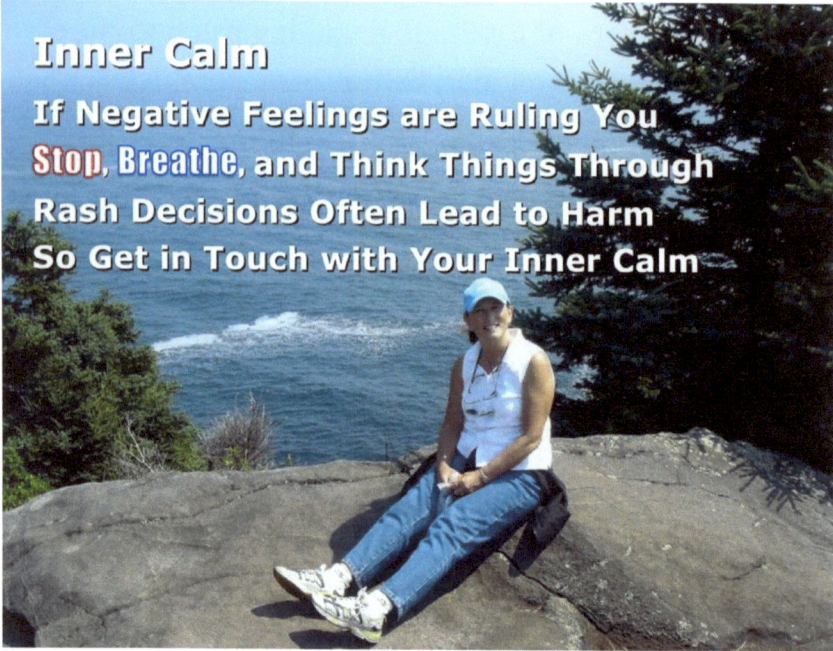

Inner Calm

If Negative Feelings are Ruling You
Stop, Breathe, and Think Things Through
Rash Decisions Often Lead to Harm
So Get in Touch with Your Inner Calm

Breathing slowly and steadily can be difficult in the beginning; keep at it. Focus on your whole physical body, in addition to your breathing. Where in your body are you holding your tension? Focus on these parts of your body. "Breathe into" each part of your body where you have tension, releasing the tension a little each time that you exhale. You may wish to use the image of the waves moving toward the shore (as you inhale), and then retreating from the shore (as you exhale) to assist you in establishing a healthy rhythm and systematic release of tension.

There is much scientific evidence to support the importance of breathing slowly, deeply, and completely as part of stress reduction. Research has shown that breathing changes the body's physiology—calming down our sympathetic nervous system's response to perceived threat. When you are under stress, continue to breathe slowly, deeply, and completely for as long as it takes until you feel calmer, in control, and ready to be constructive. If the situation allows, you may want to move to a different physical space or take a walk. Remember to keep breathing slowly, deeply, and completely. With practice, calming yourself through breathing will take much less time.

You can make better sense of your challenging situation when you are fully "emotionally present"—fully aware (i.e., "mindful") of what is happening in the present moment. Without making judgements about what is happening around you, pay careful attention, not only to your breathing, but to all of your senses. When you are in touch with your **Inner Calm** and are ready to be constructive in your attitudes and actions, it is time to begin to think things through—it is time to **Reflect** on what you will **Choose** to do next.

Making Sense of Life

Look and really see

Listen and really hear

Breathe and really smell

Touch and really feel

Take it all in

Taste Life

STEP 3: REFLECT

REFLECT

三思
案ずる
Cogita
Συλλογιστείτε
सोचो
تَفَكّر
להרהר
Endurspegla
Kutafakari
반영
Reflektere
Reflechi
Phản ánh
คิด
Réfléchissez
Reflexiona
Riflettete
Reflite
Всмотритесь
Betrachten
Razmislite
Mencerminkan
Tefekkür
Sumasalamin

Take a look in the mirror of your mind
You may be surprised at what you find
Do you get angry at the drop of a hat?
Perhaps it doesn't even take that
Do you feel caged when you're delayed?
Depressed when you're dismayed?

Take a good look inside
From this truth do not hide
Take a good look within
Now's a good time to begin

If you don't like what you see
Don't just let it be
Take a good look within
Then let change begin

R eflecting on your options is the most complex of the five-steps for staying constructive in the face of change and challenge. In this section, we encourage you to **Reflect** upon five questions about the change or challenge that you are presently experiencing:

- How much **IMPORTANCE** does this event have in my life?
- What is the **MEANING** of this event in my life?
- What **OPTIONS** do I have to change, influence, or avoid this?
- Which of my options are consistent with my **VALUES**?
- How much **EFFICACY** do I have for following through on my options?

To help you remember these questions and the preferred order for considering them, we use the **I-MOVE** acronym:

I	IMPORTANCE
M	MEANING
O	OPTIONS
V	VALUES
E	EFFICACY

I — IMPORTANCE

Use the 4-Level Alarm System described below to rate the level of change or challenge you are experiencing presently. Unless you are in a crisis situation, it is likely that you are experiencing a Level 1 or Level 2 Alarm:

Level of Alarm	Number of Alarm Bells	Description
Level 1	🔔	Something is not the way you want it to be
Level 2	🔔 🔔	A threat to your self-esteem or something that has meaning or value to you
Level 3	🔔 🔔 🔔	A threat to basic safety or security (of self or others)
Level 4	🔔 🔔 🔔 🔔	An immediate life threat (to self or others)

Alarm level also can be illustrated by the number of Red Alarm Bells, as shown above. For example, a Level 1 Alarm is associated with One Red Alarm Bell. Likewise, a Level 2 Alarm is associated with Two Red Alarm Bells, and so on. How many Red Alarm Bells best characterize your present situation with respect to change or challenge?

M — MEANING

What does this change or challenge mean to you? Are you losing, or at risk of losing, something or someone? Is something or someone new coming into your life or home? If you are able to cope successfully with this change or challenge, how would this effect your life? If you do not cope well, how would this effect your life, basic safety or security, self-esteem, or something of meaning or value to you?

It is important to take the time to think deeply about what the change or challenge means to you. Try to be honest with yourself about your thoughts and feelings. You do not have to share your thoughts and feelings with anyone else, unless you wish to share them.

O — OPTIONS

Brainstorm options for changing, influencing, or avoiding this challenging situation. You can do this on your own or, if time allows, with trusted friends or family members, or a qualified counselor.

Following are 10 questions that may help you to evaluate your options, as you try to narrow them down to the most constructive ones that are appropriate to the event or situation. Your answers to the questions are not meant to be mutually exclusive. For example, a response may be both assertive and constructive, or a response may be both hurtful and destructive.

- Is *no response* an option?
- Are any of your options *assertive*?
- Are any of your options *kind*?
- Are any of your options *harsh*?
- Are any of your options *loving*?
- Are any of your options *hurtful*?
- Are any of your options *manipulative*?
- Are any of your options *helpful* or *constructive*?

- Are any of your options *unhelpful* or *destructive*?
- Would any of your options *make matters worse*?

What is the likely EFFECT or OUTCOME of each option on your well-being and the well-being of others? Envision potential positive and negative effects, and other outcomes, of your actions. For each option, what do you expect will be the effect (or effects) of your actions? Will your actions help you stay on a constructive path or return to a constructive path, if you are not currently on one.

V — VALUES

Which of the options that you identified in the previous step are consistent with your values when you are your *best self*? Your values flow from the meaning of your life and also are influenced by your culture, your religion, your friends, your community, and your family.

E — EFFICACY

All of us can envision ourselves performing actions, and we can anticipate possible obstacles. We can ask ourselves, "Realistically, to what extent can I follow through on completing my top option(s)? Am I able to do it? Do I believe that I can successfully perform the required behaviors, including speaking to someone, if necessary? On which options can I follow through to completion?" Confidence that *you* have the ability to perform an action or set of actions successfully in a specific situation is called *self-efficacy*. You may have self-efficacy for one type of action but not for another.

For example, you may be very confident that you can be assertive with coworkers but not with your boss. You may have self-efficacy for staying cool under pressure with friends but not with your children or spouse.

Self-efficacy is influenced positively by anticipation of things that facilitate success. Self-efficacy is influenced negatively by anticipation of barriers to success. Facilitators and barriers can be practical things; they can be words or actions by others, or your own thoughts, feelings, and actions. Examples of facilitators include writing and then rehearsing what you would like to say to someone, encouragement from others, changing the environment to support your success, getting necessary tools, and making time and space. Examples of barriers include lack of social support, negative self-talk, lack of necessary tools, knowledge or skill, and lack of time or space.

STEP 4: CHOOSE

CHOOSE

抉择
决する
Sumo
Διαλέξτε
चुनो
اختار
לבחור
Velja
Kuchagua
선택
Velg
Chwazi
Chọn
เลือก
Choisissez
Elige
Scegli
Escolhe
Выбрать
Wählen Sie
Odaberite
Pilih
Seçin
Pumili

More than any animal on earth

Humans have the ability to

Reflect and choose

This gift we dare not lose

This gift we should not abuse

Whether you choose the way

of Confucius, Krishna, Buddha,

Moses, Jesus, Mohammed,

Mother Nature or "None of the Above"

We hope your way includes

Peace, Compassion, and Love

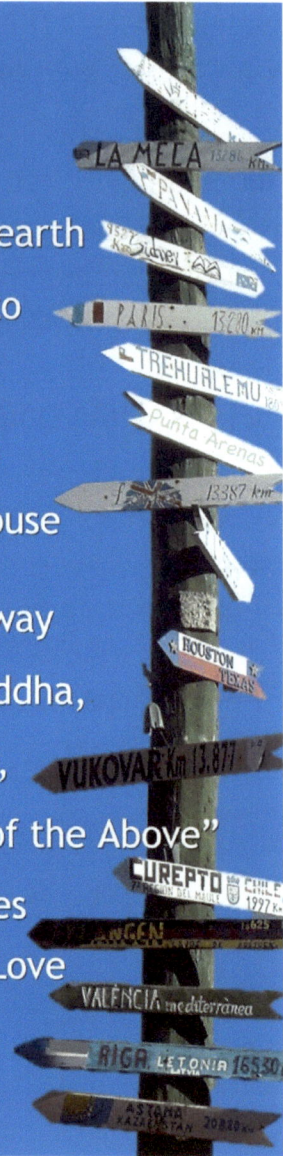

C hoose constructively! First, examine each of the options for responding that you generated in the **Reflect** step. Think about the positive and negative consequences of each option and make a realistic judgement about your ability to perform the actions needed to achieve a constructive outcome.

In addition, judge how each option is consistent or inconsistent with your values. Which one or ones will make you feel good about yourself, especially when you are your *best self*?

Second, from a rational point of view, **Choose** your most preferred course of action, while also considering what your second and third choices might be, if for some reason your first choice does not work. Whether your options are many or few, it can be useful to make a chart in order to be systematic in your evaluation.

Third, listen to your "gut" regarding your preferred options. It is important to think about your options from both rational and emotional points of view. If you have the time, you may wish to "sleep on it" before committing to your final plan of action. The best path forward is often much clearer after a good night's sleep.

Remember that when adapting to change and challenge, you are in greater control of your life when you exercise your ability to **Reflect** and **Choose**. We hope that after you have reflected on your options using **I–MOVE**, you will be in a better position to **Choose** wisely among the paths that are open to you, given the information you have.

Figuring out the best path is not always easy!

Sometimes going with the crowd seems best...

Other times you just need a little solitude...

STEP 5: ACT

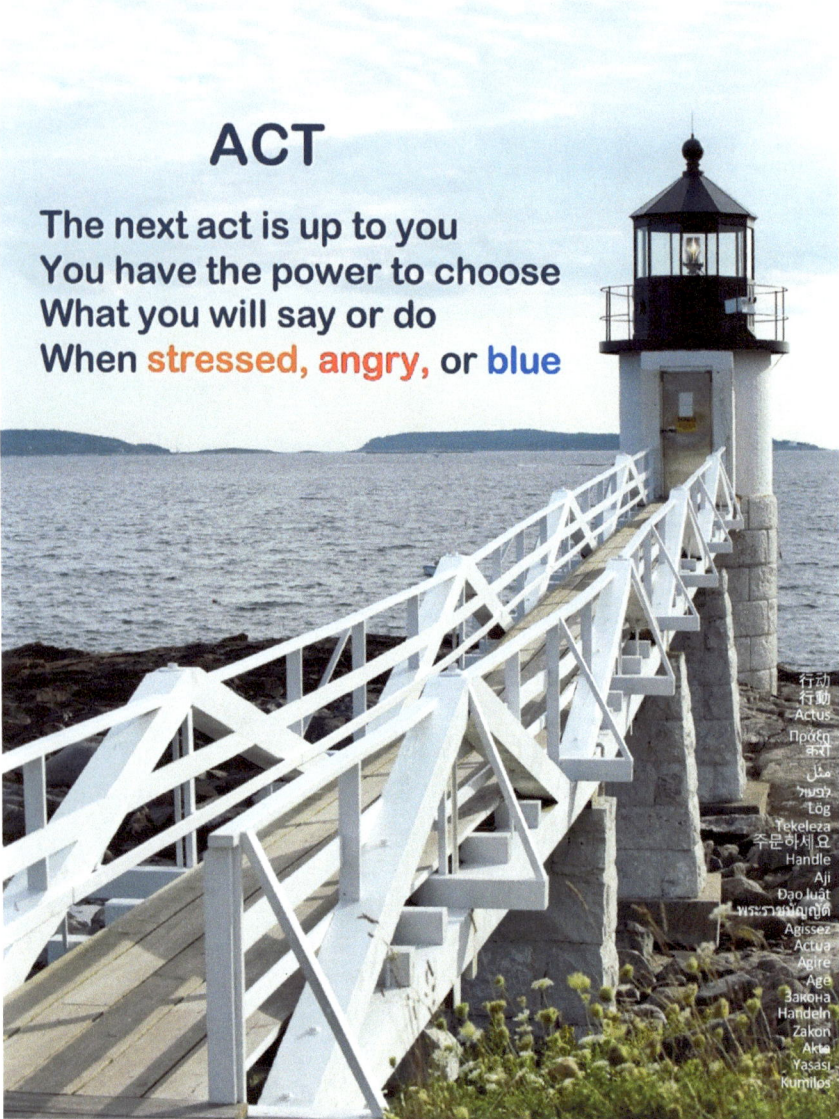

ACT

The next act is up to you
You have the power to choose
What you will say or do
When stressed, angry, or blue

Marshall Point Lighthouse Background Image © Natalia Bratslavsky|Dreamstime.com

A ct constructively! Think about how you can implement your choices in a way that will maximize the likelihood of their success, as well as enhance the well-being of yourself and others. Take time to identify, and plan strategies for overcoming, motivational barriers to your success, such as your own patterns of wishful thinking, pessimistic thinking, or passivity. Likewise, plan strategies for identifying and overcoming environmental obstacles and barriers put forth by others. Rehearse your **Acts**.

Whatever your options, we urge you to take an active role in *shaping your life* and your world. Like Johnny Appleseed did with apple seeds—you can **Choose** to sow and nurture seeds of well-being all along your path. You and your loved ones and descendants stand to share in the future harvest. You also will be modeling constructive action for others in your family, neighborhood, workplace, community, and society.

Acting constructively also means following through to explore the consequences of your actions and learning from those actions—whether or not you achieved the intended outcome. What worked and what did not work? Remember, some of the best learning is based on our mistakes, as long as we think about and **Reflect** on what we have learned. It is through thoughtful assessment, preparation, planning, and action that you overcome challenges and manage change.

THE PACT

The Marshall Point Lighthouse, shown previously and on the opposite page as the background for the poem, **The Pact**, is located in Port Clyde, Maine. Interestingly, this is the same lighthouse to which the character Forrest Gump (in the movie of the same name) ran before turning around and running in a different direction. If you are running down a dangerous or non-constructive path, there never will be a better time than the present to simply turn around and take those awkward but exciting first steps toward a more constructive path of your choosing.

We suggest that you practice using your *Seeds of Well-Being Cool Hand* and **I–MOVE** in everyday situations. For example, the next time something does not go exactly the way you want, use this opportunity to practice "getting a grip on yourself" sooner and more effectively. By practicing in everyday situations, you stand to increase your ability to stay constructive when major life changes and challenges arise. Make a **Pact** with yourself to work toward being your *best self*.

In the spirit of Gandhi,

BE the change you wish to see in the world.

— BE A SEED OF WELL-BEING —

28

THE PACT

Imagine that whenever you stumble
On a bump along your path
It seems your life might crumble
Unless you run, hide, or attack

Now imagine your surprise
When one day you realize
That a bump is only a bump
And that you have made a pact:
When you stumble, you will
Stop, Breathe, Reflect, Choose,
then ACT

Marshall Point Lighthouse Background Image © Marianne Campolongo\Dreamstime.com

seedsofwellbeing.com